D1192647

The Stewardship Series 3

LIVING ON BORROWED TIME

Principles Related to Debt

The Stewardship Series 3

LIVING ON BORROWED TIME

Principles Related to Debt

LARRY BURKETT

Edited and Arranged by Karen C. Lee-Thorp

© 1996 by
LARRY BURKETT

All rights reserved. No part of this book may be reproduced in any form without permission in writing from the publisher, except in the case of brief quotations embodied in critical articles or reviews.

All Scripture quotations, unless indicated, are taken from the *Holy Bible, New International Version®*. © 1973, 1978, 1984 International Bible Society. Used by permission of Zondervan Publishing House. All rights reserved.

Scripture quotations marked (NASB) are taken from the *New American Standard Bible* ®, © 1960, 1962, 1963, 1968, 1971, 1972, 1973, 1975, 1977, 1994 by The Lockman Foundation. Used by permission.

Edited by Adeline Griffith, Christian Financial Concepts

ISBN: 0-8024-2805-3

1 3 5 7 9 10 8 6 4 2

Printed in the United States of America

TABLE OF CONTENTS

Using This Study Guide   7

SESSION 1: The Credit Revolution   11

SESSION 2: The Real Plan   25

SESSION 3: Belonging to God   35

SESSION 4: Desires   47

SESSION 5: Belonging to Somebody Else   55

SESSION 6: Broken Relationships   65

SESSION 7: Two Alternatives   77

SESSION 8: Belonging to Each Other   87

USING THIS STUDY GUIDE

Learning to handle money and possessions is one of the most important things we can do for our spiritual growth. Our use of money both reflects and greatly affects the true state of our relationship with God. But money is a touchy subject—rarely discussed in either pulpits or small groups—so many people are simply unaware of how much insight the Bible offers into handling money wisely.

The Stewardship Series of study guides is designed to help you learn and practice the basic biblical principles of handling wealth, whether you have a lot or a very little. A *steward* is someone who manages another person's property. God has entrusted every one of us with resources to manage for His purposes. When we understand God's goals and methods, managing money can become an exciting adventure instead of a confusing burden.

Living on Borrowed Time addresses borrowing and debt. Debt is an increasing problem in our country: a cause of marital strife, emotional stress, and ruined lives. The biblical teaching on borrowing and debt—what we should and shouldn't do—is fairly straightforward. Most people can grasp the basic concepts in about an hour; but, for a great many Americans, following those clear instructions seems nearly impossible.

Why do we find it so hard to do what the Word says? This study will explore why we get into debt, why we find it hard to live biblically regarding borrowing, and how we can get on the right track.

This guide is designed with small groups in mind.

Money is an intensely private matter, and you won't be asked to divulge information inappropriately, but teaming up with a group of like-minded people offers you the chance to learn from others and receive their encouragement. However, you can easily adapt *Living on Borrowed Time* for use with just one other person or even use it on your own. If you are helping someone else learn to manage his or her finances, you may find the guides in this series to be a helpful part of what you do together. Engaged and married couples also will find these guides invaluable when sorting out how to handle their finances jointly.

The following elements are included in the sessions.

Approach Question(s). Most sessions begin with one or two questions that invite participants to share what they have been thinking and feeling about money during the week. These questions often refer to the homework assignment from the previous session. Group members have a chance to share with each other what they have learned from the homework exercise.

Teaching and Scripture. Next there are several pages of teaching on a topic, built around a few key passages of Scripture. Ideally, participants should have read and digested this section before coming to the group meeting; but, the text is brief enough to take ten minutes to read it during the meeting. Key paragraphs and Scripture passages could be reread during the meeting as a basis for discussing the questions.

Discussion Questions. These questions invite you to respond to the teaching and Scripture. Two people could probably cover them in twenty minutes; eight or ten people could use an hour, although forty minutes would be adequate. Some questions may provoke such a lively discussion that the leader will have to decide whether to cut off the discussion and move on or skip some of the later questions. When a question is personal, you always have the option of writing a full answer on your own and telling the group only what you feel is appropriate.

The Grace Adventure. Each session closes with a reminder that God's grace is available to accomplish what God's Word asks of us. God doesn't pile a lot of commands on us and leave us to fend for ourselves.

This section also includes a suggestion about how to pray in response to what you have been discussing. Prayer is a way of acknowledging and seeking God's grace. If your group is accustomed to praying together, you may not need the suggestions to guide your prayers.

If some participants are unaccustomed to praying aloud, you may decide to make your prayer time brief, allow time for silent prayer only, or let some pray aloud and others remain silent. Decide on the ground rules for group prayer at your first meeting so that no one will fear being put on the spot later on.

During the Week. A Bible study guide typically asks you to study one or more Bible passages in preparation for your next group meeting. By contrast, this guide asks you to reflect on one or two of the verses you have just discussed. The idea is to let those key truths sink into your mind and heart.

You'll also be asked to pay attention to the way you handle money during the week, in light of what you have been discussing. Meditating on Scripture and observing your own behavior work together to help you really listen to what God is telling you to do. Prayer will be a part of this listening.

Finally, you'll be asked to read the teaching for the next session. If you only have time to either read the next session or to do the other homework activities, choose the meditating and observing. However, reading ahead should take you only about ten minutes and will save a lot of time during your group meeting.

I trust that the Holy Spirit will guide you to examine your financial life through the teaching of God's Word.

* * * *

"Lay hold of my words with all your heart; keep my commands and you will live. Get wisdom, get understanding; do not forget my words or swerve from them. . . .Wisdom is supreme; therefore get wisdom. Though it cost all you have, get understanding" (Proverbs 4:4–5, 7).

THE CREDIT REVOLUTION

This study guide is about debt. During the course of this study we will address questions about debt.

- What is debt?
- Why is it so common in our society today?
- How does it affect us?
- What does the Bible say about it?
- What keeps us from getting out of debt?
- How can we respond?

This first session will give you the big picture: how debt became such a driving force in our country and how it is affecting people's lives. With that context in mind, future sessions will help you to evaluate your own situation.

But first, take a moment to get to know something about the others in your group. Money is a private subject, and debt can be embarrassing. You never will be asked in this study to reveal the details of your personal financial situation, but you will be discussing a topic that sparks strong feelings, so it helps to know a little about other group members. Give everyone in the group a chance to answer question 1 briefly. Then go around the group again, letting everyone discuss the answers.

1. Tell your name (unless everyone knows it) and one `
   thing you remember about your parents' financial or
   debt situation when you were a child. For example:

   ❑ Our family was always in debt.
   ❑ My parents never bought anything except with
      cash.
   ❑ We were rich; we had everything.
   ❑ We didn't have much, but it didn't bother me
      until I got to be a teenager.
   ❑ My parents' financial struggles made me feel
      insecure.
   ❑ Other

2. Why have you come to a group that is examining
   borrowing and debt? What do you hope to get out of
   this group?

   ❑ It's purely an intellectual exercise; I'm mildly
      interested in the topic.
   ❑ My spouse threatened to divorce me if I didn't
      come.
   ❑ Our group seems to think borrowing and debt are
      spiritual issues.

❑ I tried to get out of debt but I can't seem to manage it; I want to know what the problem is.

❑ I have a feeling God's views on debt won't make me happy, but I guess I'd like to know what they are anyway.

❑ Debt seems to be a huge issue for a lot of people I know; I'd like to understand why.

❑ I'm starting a new phase of my life and I don't want to blow it by mishandling money.

❑ Other (describe your goals)

Allow the group five to ten minutes to read the following information on their own.

A Great American Idea

If you were born after 1950, you don't remember when home mortgages were rare and car loans covered twelve months or less. In the Great Depression of the twenties and thirties, droughts ravaged farms and the bottom fell out of home and land values, so banks were forced to foreclose on many thousands of properties. Both borrowers and lenders became extremely cautious about extending and using loans. Young couples saved to buy homes, which were much less expensive because almost nobody could afford a large mortgage. Home appliances were few, and people saved cash to buy them. Home electronics were unknown.

But after the World War II, the government found itself with several million ex-GIs who needed homes, jobs, and education. Banks were reluctant to lend to so many people with virtually no credit history. So, as a last resort, the government became the lender. Congress passed the GI Bill, allowing the federal government to guarantee loans to military veterans for education and housing.

The impact on the economy was spectacular. Millions of Americans went to college, and millions more borrowed money to build homes and start businesses. The credit boom of the twentieth century was off and running. The government programs were so popular that they were soon expanded to include nonveterans through the Federal Housing Administration, the Federal Farm Loan Administration, the Small Business Administration, and so on.

Because credit stimulated demand for education, housing, and businesses, prices rose. If you're familiar with the law of supply and demand, you know that when more people are shopping for houses, sellers can sell to the highest bidder, and prices tend to rise. Further, the highest bidder was no longer the person with the most cash but the person who could borrow the most money—a considerably larger amount. Increasingly, nobody could afford a decent home, a new business, or a college education without a loan or scholarship.

Private lenders saw the demand for loans increase, so they stepped in and reaped huge profits. We'll never understand the grip that debt has on our economy unless we comprehend how much money some people are making from this system. The interest we pay on a thirty-year mortgage is easily three or four times the selling price of the house. If for a $100,000 house, $100,000 goes into the pocket of the builder and $350,000 into the pocket of the lender, the latter is strongly motivated to keep the debt system going.

By the 1970s even consumer items, such as food, clothing, medical care, and travel, depended on credit through credit cards and small loans. Lenders relaxed their requirements for qualifying borrowers because they needed to continue lending to stay in business. By the 1980s debt had become the engine that fueled the economy. If people didn't borrow to buy cars, the car companies were in trouble. If home appliance dealers didn't convince people that (a) they needed the latest appliances and (b) they could finance the payments, then home appliance dealers never could sell enough products to stay in business. The federal government had taken on so many responsibilities that it couldn't possibly maintain them without borrowing.

Ten years ago most people who were in desperate financial condition acquired their debt with loans for cars, furniture, and consumer appliances. But consider the following scenarios.

Education

According to *Money* magazine,[1] Danielle Arcaro will be fifty-three years old "by the time her federal and private lenders collect the more than $416,000 due in combined principal and interest on her $118,366 in student loans. That's despite the fact that as an ophthalmologist in private practice" she will earn $100,000 per year. Today, of the $1,900 per month she makes as a medical resident, $804.67 goes to pay off her husband's student loans for his M.A. in architecture. He won't make more than $40,000 in his field for at least a decade.

Tuition in graduate schools is rising twice as fast as inflation. An M.D. today costs about $150,000; a law degree costs $100,000. Student loans are easily available from the federal government, and private lenders compete to lend to graduate students. The offered loans are initially cheap, but their interest rates rise 2.85 to 3.5 points after graduation—usually with no cap. Graduate students like the Arcaros are mortgaging their futures. Many of their parents are taking out home equity loans to help pay for graduate school and thereby endangering their own retirements.

Computers

Open any current issue of *Time* or *Newsweek*, and you can expect to find at least one story, ad, or column touting the Internet as the must-join club of this decade. "Last one in the Internet is a silly goose" proclaims an ad for Global Village Communications, which provides Internet link services to businesses. The ad pictures a group of children hesitating before diving into a pool. The message, to both business owners and parents, is that they cannot afford *not* to "invest" in going online. Comdex '95 estimates that ten million computers will be sold in the 1995-96 fiscal year for home use; half of those will be to first-time buyers.

But what does it cost to put a family online? You easily

can find yourself dropping $5,000 at the computer store on a CPU with multimedia capabilities, monitor, CD-ROM, software, and so on. Prices for units of memory and many components are dropping, but the standard of what you "really need" to take advantage of the latest software and online services continues to rise, so the average consumer will leave the computer store spending 30 percent more than he or she would have spent last year (but with much more powerful stuff).

Computer stores have become as adept as car dealerships at providing "financing"—that is, debt. And then there's the cost of the online service. Basic service with online services is as low as $9.95 per month, but the cost quickly goes up if you send and receive much E-mail, download programs or magazine stories, enter "chat rooms" to talk online with other people (at per-minute rates), or venture out into the Internet itself. Multiply that cost several times if you want to use the World Wide Web's graphically enhanced "home pages." It's not hard to spend $300 in the first month, as many families have discovered with dismay.

But if all the kids in your child's class are online, and the media warns that computer-illiterates will be bypassed in the economy of the next century, can you afford to deny your children this necessity of life?

A Place to Belong

Bankers, credit card companies, automobile manufacturers and retailers (companies that not only build and sell cars but also offer financing), appliance manufacturers and retail stores, department stores (with their own credit cards), advertisers—all these businesses prosper only to the extent they can convince the consumers of two things.

1. In order to *belong* (to the successful middle class, the hip younger generation, or whatever group we choose), we need this or that product now, and

2. In order to obtain that product now, it is good and smart for us to borrow the money to pay for it.

The human desire to belong to some community is almost as powerful as the desire for enough to eat. Young people who feel they don't belong to our wider society or to stable families become fiercely loyal to gangs. All of us have that same urge.

How does a guy feel when all his friends drive new cars and have the latest stereo equipment? He wants the same things, if things are what defines who is "in" and who is "out." He feels he can't wait three years to save the money for a cool car, and television ads bombard him with the message that he can and should have the car now by borrowing to pay for it.

In the same way, if you believe your children will be "out of it" without Internet access, you may decide to finance the $5,000 to $6,000 it will cost you this year to put your family online. If you need a certain wardrobe to look appropriate (part of the group) at your job, then it makes sense to buy it with a credit card.

In our society, what you wear, drive, live in, sit on, or use in your free time defines who you are and whether you belong. Identity and belonging are so important to a human soul that the people who profit from our debt know they'll win if they play on those desires. But the belonging they offer is false and empty, and they don't care if we ruin our lives in the pursuit of it.

3. How would your life be better, worse, easier, or harder if the following situations were true today?

❑ If cars could be bought only with cash; banks and dealers did not loan money for cars (of course, family members could still lend money).

❑ If computers and other home office equipment could be bought only with cash.

❑ If stereos, TVs, VCRs, and other home electronics could be bought only with cash.

❑ If credit cards did not exist.

❑ If people had to have at least a 40 percent down payment before they could buy a house.

❑ If college loans and financial aid did not exist.

_____

_____

_____

_____

4. Is it hard for you to imagine a world in which most people's only line of credit was from the local butcher or grocer, and almost everything was bought with cash or not bought? Why or why not?

5. How does it make you feel to know that credit
   wasn't always a fact of life?

6. How does the advertising slogan "Last one in the
   Internet is a silly goose" play upon your desire to
   belong?

7. Can you think of other advertising messages (such
   as for clothing, children's toys, or cars) that play
   upon people's desire to be one of the gang?

8. Which of the following do you think are essentials of life that you would be unwilling to live without? Explain your reasons.

   ❏ Your own home
   ❏ A home equivalent in value to the ones owned/rented by your friends
   ❏ A personal computer
   ❏ Computer online service
   ❏ A stereo system less than four years old
   ❏ A car for each adult in your household
   ❏ At least one car in your household that is less than four years old
   ❏ Living room furniture purchased new
   ❏ Your bedroom furniture purchased new
   ❏ Your children's bedroom furniture purchased new
   ❏ Private schooling for your children
   ❏ College educations for your children

9. Do you think your desire to belong to American culture affects any of your buying decisions? If so, how? If not, why not?

_____

_____

_____

_____

The quite natural desire to belong in our society pushes us into debt because our society defines belonging by possessions. Belonging also fuels debt in another way. Because money is freely available for borrowing, the demand for homes, cars, health care, and computers rises, so prices rise also. As individuals we're helpless to do much about the economic structure of our nation. Houses cost what they cost; if you want one, you have little choice but to borrow.

If belonging to the American community is a big part of what gets us into the debt mess, then belonging to another kind of community will be a big part of what will get us out of it. In future sessions, we'll explore how Christian community offers us a way out.

10. How are you feeling at the end of this session? (Encouraged? Discouraged? Confused? Intrigued?) Why?

_____

_____

The Grace Adventure

In the Bible, *grace* refers to two generous gifts God gives us. One is the welcoming forgiveness He offers us when we fall far short of His standard for a wise and loving life. The other is the empowering presence of the Holy Spirit within us—the Spirit who can enable us to become people we never dreamed of being. Unless we believe firmly that God extends grace to us with both hands, we likely will find that studying His principles about money will produce little but guilt and rationalization. But if we believe in grace, then those same principles can become doorways to an adventure in living by grace.

11. Divide into groups of three. Tell your partners one thing that has seemed especially significant to you in this session. Then tell them one thing this session prompts you to ask from God. Finally, let each person pray for the partner on his or her right, asking for the thing that person mentioned.

During the Week

In this session we have been talking about what the Bible calls "the world"—the beliefs, customs, systems, and institutions of a society that are hostile to God. The apostle Paul understood the strength of cultural tides, and he counseled a way of resisting them: *"Do not conform any longer to the pattern of this world, but be transformed by the renewing of your mind. Then you will be able to test and approve what God's will is—his good, pleasing and perfect will"* (Romans 12:2).

Meditating on biblical truth is one way to renew our minds and transform ourselves. Copy Romans 12:2 onto a card or sheet of notepaper. Post it where you will see it often during the week—perhaps on your dashboard, over your desk, or on your refrigerator. Each time you see it, read it, and let one of the phrases roll around in your mind. What does it mean? What significance does it have for you? Take note of how it makes you feel—uncomfortable, convicted, encouraged? What is God saying to you in this verse?

Another tactic for ceasing to conform to the world's patterns is to develop the habit of noticing what the world is saying to you. Just noticing is a huge part of the battle. Watch this week for advertisements or news stories that tell you you'll be "out of it" if you don't own some product. Come to session 2 prepared to tell about one such message.

---

1. Beth Kobliner, "Facing 20 Years of Debt," *Money*, November 1995, 109.

THE REAL PLAN

1. What is one way in which you've gotten the message this week that if you want to be a good American (good parent, good member of the middle class) you had better buy this or that?

The Scam

Not only does our system reward borrowers with instant gratification, it actually penalizes people who live within their means. Cheryl, a single woman in her mid-thirties, thought she must have the ultimate credit rating because she used a credit card only for business, never carried a balance, and always paid cash for cars. She was shocked to discover that her prudent ways had given her a terrible credit rating. Her records showed no borrowing and no personal credit cards. (This is the kind of clean slate that usually indicates a person who has been through bankruptcy and cannot get credit.) With no proof that she had ever borrowed money and paid it back, she was unqualified to buy a house.

Frustrated, she decided that she would obtain a loan for her next car, even though she had saved enough money to buy the used car she wanted. So she borrowed

$10,000, intending to pay off the loan after six months (enough time to establish a credit history). When she received the loan papers in the mail, however, she discovered something the lender had failed to mention. When she paid off the loan in six months, she would be expected to pay not only the $10,000, but also the full $4,000 of interest she would have owed over the three years of the loan. The lender would reimburse most of that $4,000 within ninety days. Until then, the lender would have the use of that money, and Cheryl would have to take that much more out of her savings. She wondered whether buying a credit history was worth the hundreds of dollars it would end up costing her.

In the past fifty years we have taken a detour from the kind of free market system envisioned by Adam Smith— to say nothing of the economic principles set forth in the Bible.

The Real Plan

The Old Testament Law describes a pattern for borrowing and lending that remains revolutionary three thousand years after it was given. According to the book of Deuteronomy, God intended Israel to stun her neighbors by becoming—through integrity and generosity—the foremost lender nation in the world. The ability to lend money out of their surplus would be one of the chief signs that God was blessing His people.

"For the Lord your God will bless you as he has promised, and you will lend to many nations but will borrow from none. You will rule over many nations but none will rule over you" (Deuteronomy 15:6).

"The Lord will open the heavens, the storehouse of his bounty, to send rain on your land in season and to bless all the work of your hands. You will lend to many nations but will borrow from none" (Deuteronomy 28:12).

Because the capacity to lend came from God's goodness, not man's financial wizardry, God expected His people to lend to one another without charging interest: *"If you lend money to one of my people among you who is needy, do not be like a moneylender;* **charge him no interest"** (Exodus 22:25; emphasis added). They could charge interest to foreigners, but among themselves they were to maintain a policy of generosity. "Do not be like a moneylender," God said. Don't be like these car finance companies that charge 13 percent or credit card companies that charge 19 percent; they're only in this relationship out of greed. A moneylender of this sort doesn't care about people, only about profit. The greedier you are, the more you think belonging means owning, the happier the moneylender is.

By contrast, the wealthy in Israel were supposed to care for the needy as if they were family and help them through hard times. The lender's goal was the borrower's good, not his greed. *"If there is a poor man among your brothers in any of the towns of the land that the Lord your God is giving you, do not be hardhearted or tightfisted toward your poor brother. Rather be openhanded and freely lend him whatever he needs. . . .Give generously to him and do so without a grudging heart; then because of this the Lord your God will bless you in all your work and in everything you put your hand to"* (Deuteronomy 15:7–8, 10).

God said that if His people took this attitude, they could all but wipe out poverty (Deuteronomy 15:1–11).

He knew that if Israel pulled off this feat, the nations would be drawn to Israel's God without an Israelite having to utter a syllable of evangelism.

But the financial blessing that would enable God's people to be generous depended on their obedience to these commands. If they disobeyed and were hardhearted, tightfisted, or grudging, then they would not prosper. The last and most humiliating in a long list of consequences would be that God's people would fall in debt to unbelievers: *"The alien who lives among you will rise above you higher and higher, but you will sink lower and lower. He will lend to you, but you will not lend to him. He will be the head, but you will be the tail"* (Deuteronomy 28:43–44). When Israel became a debtor nation, the people were not to blame the non-Jews among them but rather their own refusal to follow God's system of generosity and commitment to one another.

Thus, God did not say, "Never borrow money." He foresaw that, inevitably, hard circumstances would fall on this or that family, and the family would need its neighbors' help to recover. But the goal for every household was not merely to be debt-free; it was to be in such a state of financial order that the household could lend to those around it. Imagine the following continuum.

<--->

bankrupt   indebted   debt-free   lending liberally from surplus

Sadly, the Israelites never caught God's vision. Century after century they persisted in trying to get rich by taking advantage of the poor and widows and through military conquests. But when Jesus came, He offered the same vision to His disciples: "*Give to the one who asks you, and do not turn away from the one who wants to borrow from you*" (Matthew 5:42).

"*And if you lend to those from whom you expect repayment, what credit is that to you? Even 'sinners' lend to 'sinners,' expecting to be repaid in full. But love your enemies, do good to them, and lend to them without expecting to get anything back. Then your reward will be great, and you will be sons of the Most High, because he is kind to the ungrateful and wicked*" (Luke 6:34–35).

2. What were the basic principles of the Old Testament borrowing and lending system?

3. a. What positive words do the Bible passages above use to describe good lenders?

b. What negative words do the passages use to describe those who do not lend properly?

4. Under the Old Testament system, how did God plan to use money in order to attract non-Jewish nations to Himself?

5. Why is a generous lender likely to attract unbelievers to God?

6. Why do you suppose God's people refused to obey and be generous with each other?

7. According to Jesus, how does a generous lender resemble God Himself?

These principles often are dismissed as unrealistic. "That's fine in a farm economy, but in a postindustrial economy, businesses need to be able to borrow in order to invest in equipment and workers, and nobody will lend to a business without expecting a return." Whether or not this is true, we are not talking here about business borrowing; we are talking about consumer borrowing. Until the last fifty years, no economy in the history of the world has built itself on borrowing for consumer comfort and status instead of for need or investment. The system has given some of us the highest standard of living in history. But it is a house of cards.

The most telling criticism of Jesus' words is that nobody will lend without return. That's true in an impersonal economy in which the lender cares nothing about the borrower. But developing countries and inner city neighborhoods are experimenting with a system very much like what Deuteronomy describes.

In this system someone (a wealthy investor) gives a group of people a sum of money, and together the group lends small amounts to its members to help them start small businesses. Borrowers are highly motivated to use the money responsibly and pay it back because they know and care about the other group members. They know that if they default, they are taking money their friends really need.

Consequently, the rate of default is far lower than what impersonal banks see. The original investor's money is multiplied many times for the good of the community. A lending system based on generosity and care rather than on greed works when people have a sense of belonging to and being responsible for one another.

8. Would you be less likely to default on a loan that came from a group of your friends? Why or why not?

9. a. How easy is it for you to imagine yourself becoming not only debt-free but even a generous lender to those who need help? Why is that?

b. Does the idea appeal to you? Explain.

The Grace Adventure

God is eager to bless generous, openhearted people. The miracle is, He is even eager to forgive greedy, tightfisted, self-indulgent people and to help them change if they want to. Through the wonder of grace, it is possible for us to become not only debt-free but able to lend generously.

10. Take a couple of minutes of silence for group members to reflect on what you have discussed. Let each person think about where he or she is on the continuum between being bankrupt and lending from surplus (see page 28). Ask God to enable all of you to become people who lend liberally but do not borrow.

During the Week

The promises in the Old Testament were given to Israel as a whole nation. They are not necessarily intended as promises we can "claim" as individuals living under the new covenant of Christ. However, they do describe the kinds of ways God would like to bless us as individuals and, especially, as a believing community. It is appropriate for us to ask (not demand) God to do these things for us.

Use Deuteronomy 28:12 as a matter for prayer this week: *"The Lord will open the heavens, the storehouse of his bounty, to send rain on your land in season and to bless all the work of your hands. You will lend to many nations but will borrow from none."* Copy and post it as you did after session 1.

Read this verse daily, and take a moment to ask God to bless the work of your family's hands so that you can lend to many and borrow from none. Then pray the same for the other members of your group. Since these promises were given to a community, it honors God's intent when you pray them for a community to which you belong.

If you have doubts about God's willingness or ability to bless your work in this way, tell God about your doubts. Tell Him exactly how you feel and why. Airing your doubts is often a necessary step toward being able to ask for something with genuine faith.

BELONGING TO GOD

1. Who (if anyone) do you feel pressures you to borrow money to buy things?

   ❏ Friends
   ❏ Coworkers
   ❏ Parents
   ❏ Children
   ❏ Spouse
   ❏ The church
   ❏ TV shows
   ❏ Advertising
   ❏ The pressure comes from inside of me.
   ❏ No one pressures me to borrow.
   ❏ Other sources of pressure

No Purchase Necessary

Jenny and Cal Monroe have been wanting to become more involved in their church, so they signed up to join one of the cell groups that would be forming within the next month. One evening later that week, a woman phoned, identifying herself as Lena the cell group coordinator.

"We're looking for a couple to host the first meeting of your group," Lena explained to Jenny. "Would you be willing to do that?"

Jenny groped for a response, but something akin to panic was blanking her mind. What could she say? She would rather die than have people from the church see their apartment with its dilapidated furniture. "Well, my living room isn't very big," she finally said, "I'm not sure there's room for all those people."

"There would be only eight including yourselves," said Lena.

"Still . . . I don't think so. You'd better find somebody else. I'm sorry."

Jenny could feel her cheeks burning as she hung up the phone. Nobody at church knew how they really lived because she was always careful that their clothes looked first-rate when they attended church functions. She was not about to have them be treated as Yuffies—Young Urban Failures who were past twenty-five and still working in low-paying service jobs. Now it was clear that if she and Cal were going to fit in at this church, they were going to have to get some decent furniture in their home, even if they had to stretch their credit to the limit. If she couldn't have a house, Jenny was going to make the apartment respectable. She was sure of that.

Was Jenny's concern for appearances justified? Was she wrong to think she couldn't let members of her middle-class church into her apartment? Was she wrong to use her credit card to buy clothes for her and Cal so they could maintain an image at church?

James, the brother of Jesus and one of the leaders of the Jerusalem church, felt it necessary to insist that the age of one's furniture or clothing had better have nothing to do with the way a person was treated in the church.

"My brothers, as believers in our glorious Lord Jesus Christ, don't show favoritism. Suppose a man comes into your meeting wearing a gold ring and fine clothes, and a poor man in shabby clothes also comes in. If you show special attention to the man wearing fine clothes and say, 'Here's a good seat for you,' but say to the poor man, 'You stand there' or 'Sit on the floor by my feet,' have you not discriminated among yourselves and become judges with evil thoughts?

"Listen, my dear brothers: Has not God chosen those who are poor in the eyes of the world to be rich in faith and to inherit the kingdom he promised those who love him? But you have insulted the poor. Is it not the rich who are exploiting you? Are they not the ones who are dragging you into court?" (James 2:1–6).

2. According to James, what qualified a person to belong among God's people?

_____

_____

_____

3. Suppose one Sunday you noticed two newcomers at your church: a well-dressed, well-groomed woman and another woman obviously dressed in thrift shop clothing.

a. What would you be inclined to believe about the well-dressed woman? What qualities would you tend to ascribe to her?

b. What would you tend to believe about the shabbily dressed woman? What qualities would you ascribe to her? What might you assume about her spiritual life?

c. To which woman would you be most inclined to introduce yourself first? Why?

It's common for Americans to think well-dressed people are more intelligent, disciplined, and reliable than poorly dressed people. Career advisors tell us, "Dress for the job you want, not the job you have," because appearance is everything. If you look like an executive, people will imagine you have the qualities necessary to be an executive. Salespeople who transport clients need cars that make them look successful, or their clients will think less of their products or their abilities. It is assumed that anyone who puts his or her mind to it can succeed financially, so if you don't have money you must have done something wrong. In our country, you are more likely to be considered a moral failure if people know you live in a cheap apartment, drive an old car, and wear cheap clothes than if people know you are heavily in debt.

It's easy for us to carry those same values over into the church. If you dress and live like you have plenty of money, people can more easily imagine that you are well-to-do, even if secretly you are near bankruptcy.

4. This was evidently a problem in the earliest church, or James wouldn't have bothered to mention it. Why do you suppose it's so common for us to measure each other by what we own?

_____

_____

_____

_____

5. What about your church? Would a person feel tempted to buy the right clothes or the right

furniture on credit in order to fit in there? Explain
your view.

_____

_____

_____

_____

6. What would you say to Jenny if she went to your
   church?

_____

_____

_____

_____

7. Look around the group with whom you are
   discussing this guide. What defines whether you
   belong to this group? Does what you own have
   anything to do with it?

_____

_____

_____

_____

James said, *"Has not God chosen those who are poor in
the eyes of the world to be rich in faith and to inherit the kingdom he promised those who love him?"* (James 2:5). In order
to be an insider under the world's system, a person needs
plenty of money. But, says James, to be an insider in God's
kingdom, faith is the requirement—not money.

God's kingdom is the place and time when God
reigns, when death is conquered, wars have ceased, the
evil are defeated, and people live together in harmony.
The apostle John described God's future kingdom.

*"Now the dwelling of God is with men, and he will live with
them. They will be his people, and God himself will be with
them and be their God. He will wipe every tear from their eyes.
There will be no more death or mourning or crying or pain, for
the old order of things has passed away"* (Revelation 21:3–4).

The ultimate fulfillment of the kingdom is yet to
come, but Jesus gave his followers the task of being out-
posts of His kingdom in a hostile world.

The only qualification for belonging to God's kingdom was, as James put it, to be *"believers in our glorious
Lord Jesus Christ"* (James 2:1). The things that used to
separate people are irrelevant in the kingdom.

Paul wrote, *"You are all sons of God through faith in
Christ Jesus, for all of you who were baptized into Christ have
clothed yourselves with Christ. There is neither Jew nor
Greek, slave nor free, male nor female, for you are all one in
Christ Jesus. If you belong to Christ, then you are Abraham's
seed, and heirs according to the promise"* (Galatians
3:26–29). Belonging to Christ made belonging to a race
or socioeconomic group irrelevant.

The earliest believers set themselves up as an extended family in which (unlike many families today) the members were absolutely committed to caring for each other. *"All the believers were one in heart and mind. No one claimed that any of his possessions was his own, but they shared everything they had"* (Acts 4:32).

Every person, whether dressed well or poorly, was supposed to be equally valued. When people got the idea that they belonged to the community just because they loved God, their deep need to belong would be met, and they wouldn't feel so compelled to use money or status to belong to the world. By showing favoritism, the Jerusalem church was in danger of undermining this crucial goal. How could a person break free from the lure of worldly status if the church was going to judge him or her by the same status system? It's no wonder James was so insistent.

Paul understood the community's job in the same way. His instructions in Romans are plural, addressed to groups of believers in Rome: *"Do not conform any longer to the pattern of this world, but be transformed by the renewing of your mind"* (Romans 12:2). It was not just up to the individual to no longer *"conform . . . to the pattern of this world"*; the whole group had to do it together. As individual minds were renewed, they would reinforce each other. As the group cut a different pattern, individuals would be transformed and conform to the new pattern. They were all in it together.

People like Jenny need to get the message that cell group members will be perfectly fine in their homes with old furniture, and they will be treated just the same at church no matter how they dress. Until we in the church send a consistent message that people don't need posses-

SESSION 3

sions in order to belong, we will have great trouble in helping our members to live by biblical standards regarding debt. We got into debt together, as a nation, and although it is possible for our individual families to say no to the world on our own, we will have far more success if we band together as Christians to encourage each other in saying no.

8. How would your life be different if you were absolutely certain you would be highly respected as a member of God's people no matter what clothes you wore, what car you drove, or where you lived?

We know we belong to the kingdom of God, but that often seems abstract and far away. A regular habit of prayer and Bible reading is essential to maintaining a heavenly perspective, but it's also essential to have God's people close to us, treating us with kingdom values here and now. It takes courage to stand against our culture and live frugally but debt-free. We need to applaud each other for choosing to live courageously.

9. How could this group help make the kingdom real for each other? How could you help each other

43

overcome the world's message that to belong you
have to have what everyone else owns?

The Grace Adventure

There is absolutely no way we can stand against the
world's pressure without help. But God is eager to provide
wisdom and strength to those who ask, and He also has
given us each other for support.

10. Let each person in the group pray for the person on
    his or her right. Ask God to help that person say no
    to the world's message: that to belong, to be
    successful, he or she has to own what everybody else
    owns.

During the Week

- Take some time this week to ponder this question:
  What would it take for you to feel like you belong
  to the kingdom of God day to day? What habits
  would you need to cultivate? What help would you
  need?

- Post this thought from James 2:5: *"Listen, my dear brothers: Has not God chosen those who are poor in the eyes of the world to be rich in faith and to inherit the kingdom he promised those who love him?"* What does it say to you?

DESIRES

1. Briefly tell the group about an experience with money you had when you were a child. How did it make you feel?

What Money Represents

The Monroes are having an argument. Cal Monroe arrived home shortly after Jenny's conversation with Lena and found his wife in tears. "This place looks like a thrift shop," Jenny rages. "Tonight a woman called and asked if we would be willing to host the first meeting of a cell group because we're so centrally located. What could I say to her? Like I want to have all these church people in my tiny living room that's decorated in Early Garage Sale!"

Cal tries to take the rational stance: "So what are you saying? We should walk into a furniture store tomorrow and say, 'I'll take one of those, one of those, and one of those'? You know we can't afford that."

"I know we can't afford that because we're still paying off the car *you* wanted to impress your buddies with and the computer *you* had to have."

Stung, Cal sheds his rational pose and lets Jenny have it with the list of things she had to have that they are still paying off. The fact is, the Monroes carry nearly $3,000 in debt on their credit cards and pay over $400 per month on car loans and $300 per month in student loans. A fourth of their monthly income goes to loan payments and minimum payments on their credit balances. Issues related to money spark fights in their home at least once a week.

Why so many quarrels? James has some thoughts: "*What causes fights and quarrels among you? Don't they come from your desires that battle within you? You want something but don't get it. You kill and covet, but you cannot have what you want. You quarrel and fight. You do not have, because you do not ask God. When you ask, you do not receive, because you ask with wrong motives, that you may spend what you get on your pleasures*" (James 4:1–3).

James says the fights between Jenny and Cal come from "*desires that battle within*" each of them. On the surface one might say Jenny desires furniture; Cal desires cars. However, furniture is just a means by which Jenny thinks she can get what she really desires, and a car is just a means to get what Cal really wants.

2. From what you can tell from the argument described above, what are some of Jenny's deep desires? What about Cal's?

_____

_____

_____

_____

3. Judging from the situation in their home, how strong would you say those desires are? Why do you say that?

4. According to James, why don't Jenny and Cal have
   what they want?

James goes on to say, *"You adulterous people, don't you
know that friendship with the world is hatred toward God?"*
(James 4:4). This is strong language; James is at his wit's end
with a church full of people who are driven to belong to
the world, even though they have a no-purchase-necessary
offer to belong to God. They are filling their lives with
stress by pursuing something that feels important but
really isn't.

Why do people like Jenny and Cal feel that a new car,
computer, or furniture is a matter of life and death—a
need, not just a desire? Biblical writers use the term *the
world* for a spiritual force of unbelievable potency. In biblical terms, "the world" is the whole system of institutions
built by men and women on anti-God foundations. The
world includes the lending, retail, and manufacturing
industries that benefit from our borrowing. It includes the
advertising industry that cleverly plays on our longings to

belong, to be respected, to feel successful and important. It also includes our families to the extent that they live by values that are not of God. As children, we learn a great deal about money from watching our parents, and very often we learn things that they in no way intend to teach us. "The world" interacts with the sinful, confused parts of us (what the Bible calls our "flesh") and produces deep and strong beliefs.

For instance, Jenny's parents were not Christians, but like any parents they certainly wanted to raise her to handle money wisely. The trouble was, nobody had ever taught them how to do this. Neither of them was physically or verbally affectionate, and Jenny's father was usually out of the house working, but they expressed their love for Jenny and her siblings by buying them things. Jenny always got something special on her birthday, and Christmas was always a feast of the latest toys. When Jenny graduated from high school, her parents bought her a car. From these experiences, Jenny concluded that having material things equaled being loved; someone loved you if he or she bought you things. Her parents had no idea she was learning this, but she was. Consequently, now she feels loved by Cal only if he buys her things, and sometimes when she's feeling down, she'll go to the mall and buy something to cheer herself up. Compared to feeling loved, the credit card bill is insignificant.

Also, Jenny's parents used to argue about money often. To little Jenny's ears and eyes, it appeared that her mother wanted to buy this, while her father wanted to buy that, and the argument would determine who in the family really held the power. So money came to represent power as well as love to Jenny as she grew up. When she could buy what she wanted, she felt powerful; when she couldn't, she felt trapped and angry.

Jenny's parents were solidly middle class, but Cal's parents struggled financially throughout his childhood. They didn't fight openly about money; they whispered and worried behind closed doors. To Cal it seemed that an atmosphere of anxiety and deprivation filled his house with a bitter odor that followed him wherever he went. He never could have what the other kids had and always felt left out because of his poverty. He was ashamed of his parents and ashamed of himself. He swore to himself that when he grew up he would never have to be ashamed or anxious because of poverty again.

However, Cal's first job just didn't pay enough to enable him to live the lifestyle he had always dreamed of. Something inside him felt that he would go crazy if he had to spend another ten years—maybe a whole lifetime—living deprived. So he decided (without really thinking it out consciously) that he would simply live like he were the financially secure, successful guy he wanted to be. Now, when Jenny suggests that he doesn't love her if he doesn't buy her something she wants, he feels his manhood is at stake. He is every bit as good as her and her parents, he tells himself; so he resorts to charging his purchases.

Possessions represent love and power to Jenny, but they mean manhood, success, and self-respect to Cal. For both of them, possessions seem to mean the difference between belonging and not belonging. Love, power, self-respect, belonging—these are strong desires in men and women. It's no wonder that getting out of debt doesn't feel nearly as important.

5. Take three minutes of silence to think about these
   questions: What did I learn about money and
   possessions as a kid? What do possessions represent to
   me? Love? Power? Success? Self-respect? Belonging?
   What else? Write your thoughts.

   _____

   _____

   _____

   _____

   _____

6. Share with your group whatever you feel comfortable
   sharing about your responses to question 5.

7. How do you think these things that you learned as a
   child have affected your spending habits?

   _____

   _____

   _____

8. James says, "*You do not have, because you do not ask
   God. When you ask, you do not receive, because you
   ask with wrong motives, that you may spend what you get
   on your pleasures*" (James 4:2–3). What do you think

would happen if Jenny and Cal began asking God for other ways, rather than having possessions, to get love and self-respect?

_____

_____

_____

The Grace Adventure

James goes on to say, *"God opposes the proud but gives grace to the humble"* (James 4:6). What would happen if Jenny and Cal humbled themselves before God, admitted to Him that they're trying to get what they need in the wrong ways, and asked Him for the grace to change?

9. Break up into groups of three. Tell your partners what you want from God. Then pray for each other.

During the Week

• Choose a sentence or two from James 4 to meditate on this week. Copy it. Why does it seem personally significant?

• Set aside half an hour to think further about question 5. Get some paper and write whatever you remember about your family and money. If scenes (arguments, celebrations, shopping trips) come to mind, describe them and how they made you feel. If you remember a general atmosphere, describe it.

BELONGING TO SOMEBODY ELSE

1. When you sit down to pay your bills each month, what is that experience like for you?

   ❏ No big deal. I just write the checks.

   ❏ I dread bill-paying time.

   ❏ Paying the bills makes me nuts. I let my spouse do it.

   ❏ Paying bills is a faith adventure.

   ❏ It's easier for me to pay each bill when it arrives than to let them pile up.

   ❏ I wait until the last possible day to pay each bill.

   ❏ Each month I select one bill to tear up without opening it. That's the fun part.

Bondage

A quarter of Cal and Jenny's monthly income goes to loan payments and minimum payments on their credit balances. Since another 30 percent goes to taxes and 30 percent to rent and utilities, they are left with just 15 percent for food, clothing, health care, car maintenance, gas, haircuts, gifts, entertainment, and everything else. If they sat down to calculate this budget, they would realize immediately that it's an impossible situation. Some part of each of them knows this, so they simply avoid facing the truth. Instead, they pretend that everything will work out, if life behaves itself.

Of course, life fails them constantly. Each time it does, they act shocked and fight over whose fault it is. For example, Jenny's car fails to run endlessly without upkeep; it eventually needs oil or a new water pump. Jenny is furious, as though the universe has singled her out for this affliction, and somehow it becomes Cal's fault for not taking better care of the cars. Since they have no money saved for car repairs, the expense must go onto a credit card.

A week later, Jenny gets her hair cut. She views this as a necessity since hair does grow, but Cal snaps at her for spending twenty-five precious dollars on such an extravagance. They have a tacit agreement never to get sick or to need dental care because they have no dental insurance and the deductible on their health insurance is so high. They're still paying for a stubborn sinus infection Cal had six months ago.

Because buying things represents love and power to Jenny, the financial squeeze makes Jenny feel Cal doesn't love her (or he would get a real job and take care of her properly) or God doesn't love her (or He would provide for them better). She feels trapped and helpless. She's sleeping poorly and eating more than she should. She hates feeling insecure and out of control. One day she vows never to use a credit card again until the mess is straightened out, but the next day she feels she'll go crazy if she can't buy just one new pair of shoes. She's losing respect for Cal as a man and thinking maybe it was a mistake to marry him.

Because buying things represents success and manhood to Cal, he's very attuned to Jenny's increasingly frequent insinuations: that if he were a real man he would take control of their runaway budget, solve the problems, get a better job, and support her in the manner she deserves. Whenever Cal even gets close to thinking about their financial situation head-on, feelings of shame and helplessness start to well up in him. Since he has no idea what to do with feelings like those (and certainly doesn't trust Jenny to hear about them), his survival instinct tells him to ignore the whole thing.

The more the bills pile up and Jenny worries, the more he tells himself (and her, loudly) that she whines too much, is making too big a deal of the problem, and should trust him more. His avoidance strategy is to come home from work and lose himself in sports or video games. *If Jenny doesn't stop driving me crazy,* he says to himself, *I might just walk out.*

In a sense, they're both right about each other. Jenny is right that Cal isn't taking enough responsibility, and Cal is right that Jenny whines too much and respects him too little. They are heading down a road that many have traveled before, and its possible destinations are divorce or bankruptcy or both. At some level they know this, and it is their firm belief that they have no other alternatives. That has scared them into closing their eyes.

Jenny and Cal are in bondage. Externally, they are in bondage to their creditors. Proverbs 22:7 says, *"The rich rules over the poor, and the borrower becomes the lender's slave"* (NASB). In ancient times this was literally true. Debtors who could not pay their debts became the creditors' slaves, and all families and goods became the creditors' property. Our laws are more lenient, but the Monroes could lose their cars if they default on loans; and interest on their other bills will continue to rise unless they declare bankruptcy or find some other solution.

Internally, Jenny and Cal are in bondage to their desires; to their anger at themselves, each other, and God; and to their fear. They feel unable to stop the overspending, the fights, the sleepless nights, the undisciplined eating and video game playing, and the slide toward divorce. The apostle Paul was all too familiar with this experience of inner slavery.

"We know that the law is spiritual; but I am unspiritual, sold as a slave to sin. I do not understand what I do. For what I want to do I do not do, but what I hate I do. And if I do what I do not want to do, I agree that the law is good. As it is, it is no longer I myself who do it, but it is sin living in me. I know that nothing good lives in me, that is, in my sinful nature. For I have the desire to do what is good, but I cannot carry it out. For what I do is not the good I want to do; no, the evil I do not want to do—this I keep on doing. Now if I do what I do not want to do, it is no longer I who do it, but it is sin living in me that does it.

"So I find this law at work: When I want to do good, evil is right there with me. For in my inner being I delight in God's law; but I see another law at work in the members of my body, waging war against the law of my mind and making me a prisoner of the law of sin at work within my members. What a wretched man I am! Who will rescue me from this body of death? Thanks be to God—through Jesus Christ our Lord!" (Romans 7:14–25).

Satan is not stupid. He has managed to enslave Cal and Jenny externally to the world system of borrowing and internally to their desires, anger, and fear. They would have no trouble crying out with Paul, *"What a wretched man [or woman] I am! Who will rescue me from this body of death?"* What they need most is the hope that through Jesus Christ, rescue is available.

2. What is Cal feeling?

_____

_____

_____

_____

3. What is Jenny feeling?

_____

_____

_____

_____

4. In what ways are they experiencing slavery or bondage?

_____

_____

5. How does Paul describe the experience of inner slavery in the passage from Romans?

6. In what ways are Cal and Jenny doing what Paul describes?

7. Can you identify with Cal, Jenny, or Paul in any ways? How?

According to the National Foundation for Consumer Credit, if your total monthly payment on car loans, credit cards, and other financing (not including home mortgage) exceeds 20 percent of your income, you may well be in over your head. I would say that if you're anywhere near 20 percent, you're probably feeling pressure.

8. a. Take a minute to add up approximately what you pay each month on car loans, credit cards, and other financing. Then estimate how much of your monthly income goes to those payments. A tenth? A fifth? Somewhere in between? More? Write down your guess. You need not share it with the group.

  b. Now tell the group what it felt like to do that rough calculation. Was it easy or hard? Comfortable or uncomfortable? Does it give you a headache or bother your stomach? How close do you think your guess is to the real amount you're spending on debt?

You can skip some or all of questions 9 through 11 if you're running out of time.

9. Why is it so tempting for Jenny to blame Cal for their financial situation?

61

10. Why is it so tempting for Cal to ignore the problem?

11. What do you think Jenny would do if someone told her, "Jesus Christ offers a solution to your financial troubles"? What do you think Cal would say?

The Grace Adventure

Cal and Jenny didn't get into their mess without help from their parents, our culture, car dealers, and store owners. They won't get out of their mess without help either. They need God's help, as well as help from some of His people who are knowledgeable and caring. But it's up to them to face the truth about their situation; admit it to themselves, God, and those caring people; and take responsibility for getting out of the mess. Blaming each other, God, or society won't get them anywhere. As James said, "*God opposes the proud,*" who blame everybody else, but He "*gives grace to the humble,*" who admit the truth, take responsibility, and ask for help (see James 4:6).

12. Break into groups of three. Is there anything you'd like to admit to your partners? If so, do it. Is there anything you'd like them to pray for? If so, ask them.

This session's "During the Week" exercise will likely raise some potent emotions. You may want some encouragement along the way. If your schedule is busy, schedule some telephone or face-to-face time with someone in the group.

During the Week

- Check the guess you made in question 8. If you're married, do it together with your spouse. Take a calculator or pencil and paper, and add up how much you spent last month on car loans, credit cards, and other financing. Then divide that number by your monthly income. If the result is more than .15 (15 percent), you should be concerned. If it's more than .20 (20 percent), you should be very concerned.

- Now take a moment to pay attention to what you're feeling. Panicked? Relieved? Numb? Are you

63

holding your breath, clenching your teeth, or sweating? It's very important that you let yourself feel whatever you're feeling, since burying your feelings will make it harder for you to make good decisions later on. This is not a time for rushing to solve the problem; this is a time for letting yourself come to terms with the problem (if there is one).

The best thing to do is talk to God. *"Lord, I have a problem and I need your help. I can't make it without you, but I know that* **'I can do everything through [Christ] who gives me strength.'** *"* (See Philippians 4:13.)

Our bodies are designed with certain survival mechanisms, and one of them is that when we are frightened or angry, the higher rational areas of our brains go dormant. This enables us to react quickly to the threat of being killed, but it is not helpful in financial decision making. Since buried fear and anger can affect our brains in the same way, it's important to let them surface and dissipate before we try to solve problems.

- Call someone in your group or another person you know who will encourage you. You don't have to tell that person exactly how much debt you're carrying, but take a few minutes to talk about how it felt to look those numbers in the face. You may be doing your friend a favor by encouraging him or her to look at his or her debt situation.

- Romans 7:24–25 may be helpful for you to meditate on. Paul understood frustration and desperation. Rescue is available!

Session 6
BROKEN RELATIONSHIPS

1. What was it like for you to calculate the amount of debt you are carrying?

_____

_____

_____

Debt and Credit

Most of us are concerned with how being in debt affects us: worry, marital stress, insomnia, limited lifestyle, and other symptoms of bondage. However, the Scriptures invite us to consider how our debt affects others—the people to whom we owe money. From a biblical point of view, debt and credit are about relationships between persons. It's easy to lose sight of this in our modern society, but once we grasp this truth, then the rest of what the Bible says about debt makes sense.

First some definitions. For the purposes of our discussion, *debt* is a condition that exists when one or more of the following is true.

   (a) Payment is past due for money, goods, or
       services that have been purchased.
   (b) The total value of unsecured liabilities exceeds

total assets; if you had to cash out at any time, there would be a negative balance on your account.

(c) The household's basic needs are not being met because of past or present buying practices.

Credit is not the same as debt. Credit is a mutual trust relationship between a lender and a borrower (or potential borrower). Credit is a contract: I give you an item, and you agree to pay me for it within thirty days. Or, I give you an item because you sign a credit card receipt, a contract that your card company will pay me and you will pay your card company according to the rules of your contract with them. The use of credit becomes debt when you fail to pay your card company within the grace period and the company begins to charge you interest.

A home mortgage, then, is credit as long as you make the payments each month and as long as the value of the house exceeds the amount of the mortgage. The mortgage contract defines a relationship between you and the lender. You give your word that you will pay a certain amount each month. If you break your word, the lender gets your house instead of the money you owe.

The same would be true for a car loan, except that cars lose value so quickly after leaving the dealership that the value of the car is often lower than the value of the loan. Computers, appliances, electronics, and furniture lose even more value when they leave the stores. In general, it is foolish to borrow money for items that lose value.

As we saw in session 2, the biblical plan was for lenders to lend out of generosity and out of care for the needy; and people borrowed only in desperate circumstances. It was not customary to borrow money to buy a house, let alone furniture. Because borrowers were desperate and lenders were supposed to be motivated by generosity, they were not supposed to charge interest. In our day, however, lending is a business, and most lenders lend only in order to make a profit by collecting interest. Lenders don't typically think of themselves as having personal relationships with borrowers, and they tend to be unconcerned for the borrower's well-being.

Because Cal, Jenny, and the rest of us don't know our creditors personally and don't believe our creditors care about us as persons, we tend not to care about our creditors either. The only reason we pay our debts is because we fear the consequences if we don't. But fear is a poor motivator; it doesn't keep us from accumulating more debts.

However, we are not just doing business with faceless institutions that can afford to write off our debts if necessary. Real people have deposited their money in the bank that lent money for Cal's car. If he defaults on that loan, the bank will get the car but will not be able to sell it for the full amount of the loan. The bank will have to bear the loss. If enough of the bank's creditors default, the bank will go under. This is what happened to many savings and loan institutions in the 1980s, when foolish and unscrupulous lenders lent to borrowers who didn't care about the people who had invested in the banks. It cost average American people billions of dollars to bail out those institutions.

Likewise, if the Monroes default on their credit card debts, it won't be the card companies that suffer. When defaults increase, lenders simply raise interest rates so that those who do repay debts cover the costs of those who don't. If Cal and Jenny don't do something about their financial situation, they are in danger of cheating the many people to whom they have made promises.

As Christians, we are bound not only by the civil law but also by our word. When we borrow, we have made a promise to a real group of people whose livelihood depends on our integrity. Overdue bills signify broken promises. Making plans to pay our bills signifies that we are nurturing relationships that matter to us. Lenders are our neighbors, and God calls us to love our neighbors as much as we love ourselves.

"Do not withhold good from those to whom it is due, when it is in your power to do it. Do not say to your neighbor, 'Go, and come back, and tomorrow I will give it,' when you have it with you" (Proverbs 3:27–28 NASB).

When we understand how highly God values relationships among neighbors, it makes sense that people who fail to pay their debts are wicked: *"The wicked borrows and does not pay back, but the righteous is gracious and gives"* (Psalm 37:21 NASB). This psalm envisions the continuum we discussed in session 2 but adds the contrast of wicked versus righteous.

wicked   **righteous**

←——→

bankrupt   indebted   debt-free   lending liberally from surplus

This strong language about wickedness is meant to emphasize the point that borrowers should take their relationships very seriously. Businesspeople know the

value of a good reputation; we need to cultivate the attitude that being trustworthy is essential.

Unfortunately, in a day when cheating on tests and tax
returns is commonplace and finding a loophole in a contract is the mark of a talented lawyer, few of us cringe at
the thought of breaking our word. Furthermore, we know
that many lenders are simply out to get rich by taking
advantage of our poor spending habits, so it's tempting to
repay their wickedness with wickedness. But that turns
out to be a foolish strategy for dealing with wickedness in
the long run. Things just get worse.

If we're really mad at the debt system in our country,
we should be part of the solution, rather than adding to
the problem. Paul writes, *"Do not be overcome by evil, but
overcome evil with good"* (Romans 12:21). The best strategy for fighting an unjust debt system is to pay off our debts
and deal with the root causes of our indebtedness so we'll
never be caught in the system again.

If Jenny and Cal began to view each bill as evidence of
a personal relationship, and if they searched in their
hearts for the capacity to care about the people at the
other end of that relationship, then they might find that
love for these neighbors would prove to be a stronger
motive than fear for straightening out their finances.
Jenny might discover that money really is about love and
power—not so much about her power to get love but
about her power to give it. Cal might discover that
money really is about manhood and respect—about
whether he is a courageous enough man to treat his creditors with respect. By taking their borrowing relationships
seriously, they will demonstrate that they really do belong
among their neighbors.

2. Why is debt equivalent to breaking a promise?

3. One of the two great commandments is *"Love your neighbor as yourself"* (Matthew 22:39). What do you think about the idea that your creditors are neighbors with whom you have real relationships?

We can think of relationships as a set of concentric circles. Some relationships are closer and more intimate than others. Closest in may be our family; our best friends may be next; then our more casual friends, our coworkers, and so on. More distant relationships include the clerk at the gas station and the local librarian.

The diagram below shows the people to whom Cal and Jenny owe money, along with the amounts owed. It also shows how close Cal and Jenny feel to each of their creditors. Their doctor is certainly not a close friend, let alone family, but they do think of her as a person they know. They have somewhat less personal relationships with their mechanics (they changed mechanics when they found themselves unable to pay mechanic #1). And they think of their card companies and car loan company as faceless entities with whom they have only impersonal relationships.

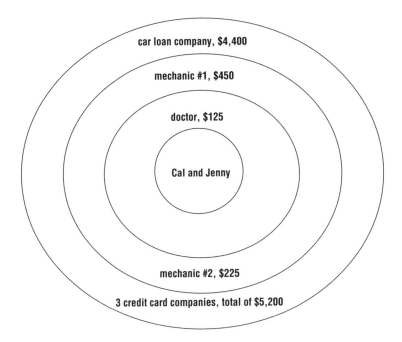

It's not surprising, then, that Cal and Jenny feel more responsible for paying their doctor than their card companies, even though they owe their card companies more and are paying more interest there. However, what would happen if they began to relate to their card companies as if those companies were made up of neighbors? They might phone the customer service departments of each of those companies and find a real, live person at the other end of the phone. They may find this person eager to negotiate a payment schedule that will work for everyone. Card companies much prefer to negotiate delayed payments than to lose an entire debt when a cardholder declares bankruptcy.

The customer service representative might politely ask the Monroes to stop using their credit card and treat them with respect. It's remarkably easy to phone a creditor and ask to speak to customer service. This neighbor-to-neighbor respectful negotiation is the essence of what the Bible urges borrowers to pursue. In such an atmosphere, Jenny can relax and Cal can feel like a man.

4. Take a few minutes on your own to list any persons or companies you owe and approximately how much money you owe to each.

_____

_____

_____

_____

_____

_____

5. On page 71 you'll find a set of concentric circles. Write the names of your creditors on that diagram, showing which ones feel closer to you and which ones seem less like personal relationships, as we did for Cal and Jenny above.

6. Why do some creditors seem more like neighbors than others?

_____

_____

_____

_____

7. What do you feel when you think about phoning one of your creditors and negotiating a payment schedule? (For example, does that feel appealing, embarrassing, or horrifying?) Why?

_____

_____

_____

_____

8. What do you think about the notion that not paying one's debts is "wicked"? Does that language seem unreasonable?

_____

_____

_____

_____

People did not use written contracts in Jesus' day, but they had a system of oral contracts based on oaths. The idea was that swearing by something religious would prove that you meant to keep your promise, for otherwise you'd be in trouble with God. It was supposedly a worse sin to break a sworn promise than just a promise. But Jesus rejected that idea. He said, *"Again, you have heard that it was said to the people long ago, 'Do not break your oath, but keep the oaths you have made to the Lord.' But I tell you, do not swear at all: either by heaven, for it is God's throne; or by the earth, for it is his footstool; or by Jerusalem, for it is the city of the Great King. And do not swear by your head, for you cannot make even one hair white or black. Simply let your 'Yes' be 'Yes,' and your 'No,' 'No'; anything beyond this comes from the evil one"* (Matthew 5:33–37).

9. Jesus says a promise is a promise—oath or no oath, whether you'll get sued or not. Why do you think He says anything less than that *"comes from the evil one?"*

10. What would it look like on the concentric circles if you loved those to whom you owe money?

74

The Grace Adventure

All this talk of "the wicked" and "the evil one" can feel intimidating—like God is waiting to strike you down if you don't live up to your promises. The truth is that Jesus died to reconcile us to God in the midst of our wickedness. The Holy Spirit offers to give us the courage to pick up the phone and talk to our creditors as fellow humans and neighbors. All we have to do is take advantage of this grace.

11. Divide into groups of three. Pray for the person on your right, asking God to forgive any past broken promises regarding money and to give this person the courage to honor each money relationship in his or her life right now.

During the Week

• Copy Proverbs 3:27 onto a card: *"Do not withhold good from those to whom it is due, when it is in your power to do it"* (NASB). Set aside some time to pray over this verse and the concentric-circle diagram of your borrowing relationships you made on page 71. Put the diagram and the verse in front of you, and read through each. Think about what it will require of you to do good to each of these persons or groups. Ask God what you should do. Pray for each of your creditors, envisioning them as real people.

• One of the key phrases in this verse is *"when it is in your power to do it."* Sometimes we underestimate our power to do good. Session 7 will address this issue.

TWO ALTERNATIVES

1. What thoughts, feelings, or pictures come to mind when you think about the word sacrifice?

Sacrifice

For those of us who, like Cal and Jenny, have a pattern of spending beyond our means and are consequently in debt, there are basically two alternatives. Unfortunately, both involve sacrifice. We can choose to sacrifice our relationships with our neighbors or creditors, or we can sacrifice some of our standard of living for a time.

It's increasingly common for Americans to choose the first alternative and opt for bankruptcy. The Bankruptcy Act of 1978 streamlined administration of the bankruptcy courts and also made personal bankruptcy much more attractive to individuals, especially because it increased the amount of assets that could be exempt from liquidation. In 1978 there were about 50,000 personal bankruptcies in the U.S. In 1988 there were nearly 500,000. Assuming this trend continues, we can realistically expect to see a million bankruptcies each year by the year 2000.

Those statistics spell trouble for many small merchants and for the credit industry as a whole. Each time another family files for bankruptcy, it thinks it is getting off free. The truth is that merchants, hospitals, and card companies either shoulder their losses or pass the costs on to other shoppers, patients, and cardholders. And with no incentive to change its spending habits, the family often ends up in debt again a few years later.

Our modern bankruptcy laws are intended to reflect the generous and loving relationships established in Old Testament law. The book of Deuteronomy states, "*At the end of every seven years you must cancel debts. This is how it is to be done: Every creditor shall cancel the loan he has made to his fellow Israelite. He shall not require payment from his fellow Israelite or brother, because the Lord's time for canceling debts has been proclaimed*" (Deuteronomy 15:1–2).

That seventh year, or Sabbath year, was also supposed to be a year of rest for the farmland and all hired help: God promised to provide so abundantly for six years that in the seventh year everybody could take a year off from agricultural labor (Leviticus 25:1–7). After seven of these Sabbath years (forty-nine years), the fiftieth year would be another year of rest, when all land that had been sold in order to pay debts would revert to the family that had owned it. This system was designed to reduce the natural tendency of wealth to accumulate in the hands of an upper class. So all loans were for six-year terms only, and all land sales were really leases of up to forty-nine years.

This system would have worked if the Israelites had taken their neighbor relationships seriously. No one would have taken advantage of lenders because lenders were neighbors, and no lenders would have taken advantage of borrowers either. However, Israel ignored the system for almost its entire history as a nation because everybody was more concerned for themselves than for their neighbors. The prophets record that this refusal to behave as neighbors was the main reason God destroyed the nation and sent its citizens into exile.

In the same way, a generous bankruptcy system would work in our country if each borrower had a strong personal sense of responsibility. Then borrowers would resort to bankruptcy only when they were truly in need of generosity. People wouldn't borrow the way the Monroes did, in order to buy the things that made them feel loved, powerful, successful, or part of the crowd. And people wouldn't default on debts unless even reasonable sacrifice wouldn't enable them to pay.

In the verse, *"Do not withhold good from those to whom it is due, when it is in your power to do it"* (Proverbs 3:27 NASB), the phrase *"when it is in your power"* becomes the sticking point for many people. The average family filing for bankruptcy owes only about $4,000. But it's usually many small, overdue bills that would require the family to endure at least two years of financial sacrifice in order to pay them. These families can file for bankruptcy, and if their creditors fail to appear in court, the court judges that the creditors have chosen to forgive the debts. In reality, it costs creditors so much to appear in court that, unless the debt is large, they are better off waiving their rights. Thus, a person who reads *"when it is in your power"* and interprets the phrase as "when it requires no decrease in your standard of living" ends up violating his or her relationships with creditors.

Sacrifice is never pleasant. If it were, we wouldn't get into debt in the first place. When first presented with the prospect of buying no new clothing for one year, Jenny rejects it as unthinkable. What if all of her hose get runs? What if she gains ten pounds and nothing fits? However,

when allowed to explore her feelings in a safe environ-
ment for awhile, she admits what really scares her is giving
up the pleasure of going to work in a new outfit, risking
the scorn of people who see her in last year's fashions, and
facing the boredom of wearing the same clothes week after
week. In biblical times, possessing three or four changes of
clothing signified wealth, but in our culture, Jenny fears
looking poor with fewer than ten winter work outfits (plus
jeans, plus . . .). Jenny will have to find a way to feel loved
that has nothing to do with the shopping mall.

For Cal, the commitment to bring his lunch to work
rather than eating fast food with the guys will be embarrassing. He knows the guys will see his homemade sand-
wich as unmanly and uncool. In order to maintain this
commitment over the long haul, Cal will have to be con-
vinced that keeping promises to his neighbors is more
manly than eating out, no matter what his coworkers
think. He will have to find his self-respect in something
other than material success, or it will drive him crazy to
give up buying any new CDs for two years.

Perhaps it will help the Monroes to go back to the root
meaning of *sacrifice*: an offering to God that expresses
worship. Under the Old Testament system, people sacrificed their best animals to God as a vivid sign that they
acknowledged Him as being first in their lives. "*Gather to
me my consecrated ones, who made a covenant with me by
sacrifice*" (Psalm 50:5). We are "*consecrated ones*" if we are
set apart and dedicated to God's service. A covenant is an
agreement of relationship; the sacrifice is the sign of
agreed relationship between God and humans.

God goes on to say that He doesn't need our sacrifices
for His own well-being: "*I have no need of a bull from your*

stall or of goats from your pens, for every animal of the forest is mine, and the cattle on a thousand hills" (Psalm 50: 9–10). Yet He urges His people to offer sacrifices for their own sake: *"Sacrifice thank offerings to God, fulfill your vows to the Most High, and call upon me in the day of trouble; I will deliver you, and you will honor me. . . .He who sacrifices thank offerings honors me, and he prepares the way so that I may show him the salvation of God"* (Psalm 50:14–15, 23).

To give up new clothes, CDs, or restaurants for two years in order to love our neighbors is a powerful act of worship toward God. It isn't quite the same as a "thank offering" (which was an expression of thanks for blessing), but it is not far off. And those who have made this kind of sacrifice relate that it does prepare the way for God to show them His salvation (deliverance).

With tears, a single father decides to forego Christmas spending this year in order to help pay off his debts. The news comes hard to his teenage daughters. Is it an admission of failure or a step of real success? Is it a concession to a cruel God who makes debtors suffer, or is it an act of worship to a God who takes covenant relationships seriously? *"The sacrifices of God are a broken spirit; a broken and contrite heart, O God, you will not despise"* (Psalm 51:17).

2. Why do you think more than half a million households declare bankruptcy each year in the U.S.?

3. a. What spiritual benefits can come from sacrifice, according to Psalm 50?

    b. How can sacrifice prepare *"the way so that I may show him the salvation of God"*? (Psalm 50:23)

4. What does the sacrifice of *"a broken and contrite heart"* (Psalm 51:7) have to do with financial sacrifice in order to pay off debts?

"Do not withhold good from those to whom it is due, when it is in your power to do it" (Proverbs 3:27 NASB). It is between each household and God to decide what sacrifices are within their power and what sacrifices are unreasonable. God doesn't ask us to sacrifice genuine *needs*, such as food, warmth, shelter, safety, jobs, and so on. He may ask us to sacrifice *wants*, however. Wants can feel like needs when they seem to be our only source of emotional things like love, self-respect, and pleasure. It's especially difficult for parents to discern which expenses for children are essential to their well-being and which can be sacrificed temporarily in order to free the family from debt.

5. Which of the following would you be willing to do without for two years in order to become debt-free? Which would you not do without and why? (Add your own items to the list and discuss them with your group. This list is intended merely to spark your thinking.)

- ❏ New CDs
- ❏ Restaurant meals
- ❏ New clothing
- ❏ Children's after-school activities that cost money
- ❏ Vacations
- ❏ In-theater movies and entertainment events
- ❏ A second car in the family
- ❏ New electronics
- ❏ Perms and hair coloring

❑ Christmas gifts, tree, decorations
❑ Other expenses

6. What is one thing you spend money on that you don't need for survival but that is very important to you? Why does it feel so important?

7. Sacrificing will mean that Jenny and Cal must seek to feel loved and respected in ways other than by spending money. Where do you think the Bible would tell them to go for love and self-respect?

8. What is going through your mind after all this discussion of sacrifice?

_____

_____

_____

The Grace Adventure

When we commit to honoring debt relationships, God will respond with grace by providing the love, respect, food, and shelter that we need. Sacrifice won't be easy, but help is available.

9. Divide into groups of three. Tell your partners one thing you would like God to help you with regarding sacrifice. Pray for each other.

During the Week

Copy Psalm 50:23 onto a card: "*He who sacrifices thank offerings honors me, and he prepares the way so that I may show him the salvation of God.*" Take some time this week to think about this verse. What do you think about honoring God through sacrifice?

Christian Financial Concepts has many resources, such as *The Financial Planning Workbook* (Chicago: Moody Press; available also from Christian Financial Concepts, Gainesville, Georgia) to help you through the practical details of devising a budget that will get you out of debt. You might want to visit your Christian bookstore and pick up one of these this week, so that if you have any questions about it you can bring those to the group next week.

The key to sacrifice is distinguishing needs from wants. As you buy things this week, ask yourself, "Is this a need or a want? If I were prepared to sacrifice could I get by on something less expensive? How would that feel?"

In session 8 be prepared to talk about what it was like for you to think about needs and wants when you made buying decisions.

BELONGING TO EACH OTHER

1. What was it like for you this week to ask yourself, "Do I *need* this or do I merely want this?" when you made buying decisions? If you forgot about doing this, how do you think you would have felt in the mall or the grocery store having to discern needs versus wants?

The Process

According to the American Banker's Association, delinquent loans at the end of 1995 were at their second highest level since 1985. The rate of overdue loans had risen steadily for four quarters in a row. The average amount owed had almost doubled since 1990. The bankers attributed this explosion of debt to two factors: lenders had become more lenient and were offering (even pushing) credit cards enthusiastically; and more businesses (even grocery stores and doctors) were now accepting credit cards. Since wages were not rising, many analysts considered it inevitable that there eventually would be an eruption in personal bankruptcies, tighter credit, and an economic plunge.

This cycle of spiraling debt and periodic bursts of bankruptcies has been increasing during the past few decades. As individuals we can't do much about how it affects our national economy. What we can do is take ourselves out of the cycle. When we hear news reports that economic growth depends on strong consumer spending, we can turn our televisions off and go about the business of building a community whose survival does not depend on spending. When we read an ad that tells us we will be left out if we don't buy its product, we can close the magazine and return to building a community where belonging doesn't depend on buying.

Where can we find such a community? Who would join it? Ideally every follower of Christ would want to belong to a community like that, but you can start with the people in your group. Having come this far in your study of debt, you are probably just beginning to realize the risks and sacrifices involved in getting in and staying out of debt. It could be a multiyear process of disentangling yourself from the world's ways of thinking about money, separating needs from wants, changing your buying habits, and treating your creditors differently. You are going to need help. Why not help each other?

In this last session I want to invite you to consider forming an ongoing support group for people who want to get out of debt and stay out. The ground rules might look something like the following.

Time: Meet sixty to ninety minutes once a week (you can modify this to suit your needs).

Agenda: Use a resource like *The Financial Planning Workbook* (Chicago: Moody Press; available also from Christian Financial Concepts, Gainesville, Georgia or your local Christian bookstore). This workbook can help you with the nuts and bolts of budgeting. This support group, however, would be a place for you to share how you are doing at sticking to your budget, how it feels to say no to your kids, how difficult it is to distinguish needs from wants, and so on.

This is a place to share your frustrations and victories and to receive encouragement. In this place, if nowhere else, you can reinforce in each other the values of sacrifice, respect for creditors as neighbors, and respect for each other regardless of what you own.

Each week you might begin by checking in; each group member would have up to five minutes to answer a general question, such as "How did you do this week in your process of becoming debt free?" Then in your remaining time, members would be able to elaborate on their questions, frustrations, triumphs, and need for help.

"But encourage one another daily, as long as it is called Today, so that none of you may be hardened by sin's deceitfulness. . . . And let us consider how we may spur one another on toward love and good deeds. Let us not give up meeting together, as some are in the habit of doing, but let us encourage one another—and all the more as you see the Day approaching" (Hebrews 3:13; 10:24–25).

Respect: Our culture gives people respect based on what they can buy. This group needs to provide a place where people experience respect with no purchase necessary. Disrespect can be subtle; the rest of these guidelines are designed to foster respect. *"Be devoted to one another in brotherly love. Honor one another above yourselves"* (Romans 12:10).

Confidentiality: Ideally, this group will become a safe

place in which group members can be candid about their financial situations. It is crucial that all members prove themselves to be trustworthy. Absolutely nothing divulged in the group, whether facts or feelings, may be repeated outside the group. It is okay to discuss your own situation outside the group, but it is not okay to talk about other members unless they are present. If someone misses a meeting and wants to be brought up to date, it is important that he or she talk to each group member about that person's story. Strict confidentiality is a key to building trust. "A gossip betrays a confidence; so avoid [anyone] who talks too much" (Proverbs 20:19).

Honesty: The more you know each other, the more comfortable you will be discussing your private financial issues. In the beginning you will want to be more general, as you have been in this group. It is never necessary to divulge more than feels comfortable, but it is essential that everything you do say is the truth. It is not helpful to pretend everything is going well when it isn't. Two kinds of people can derail the group process. One is the person who pretends and says little. The other is the exhibitionist who treats the group as a forum for expounding all the details of his or her life. Strive for some balance of appropriate openness. "Instead, speaking the truth in love, we will in all things grow up into him who is the Head, that is, Christ" (Ephesians 4:15).

Nonjudgmentalism: Respect failure and those who are honest about failure. The goal of a group like this is to help its members grow and change. People change best in a nonjudgmental atmosphere. It is important for everyone to feel safe sharing missteps and negative emotions without getting the message that failure is shameful. We all will "blow it" repeatedly on the way to success. So whether you have made an honest mistake or actually have committed a sin, you need this group to respect your willingness to tell the truth about yourself. *"Therefore let us stop passing judgment on one another. Instead, make up your mind not to put any stumbling block or obstacle in your brother's way. . . . Accept one another, then, just as Christ accepted you, in order to bring praise to God"* (Romans 14:13, 15:7).

Advice: *Give no advice unless requested.* This is difficult for a lot of us, but advice is often disrespectful. Although other group members' feedback on how to handle a situation is frequently helpful, each person needs to take responsibility for his or her own decisions. Unfortunately, some people find it an irresistible temptation to "fix" other people's lives. It is always easier to fix other people's problems than to address our own. Therefore, the group must strictly enforce this rule to rein in advice-givers. *"When pride comes, then comes disgrace, but with humility comes wisdom"* (Proverbs 11:2).

Attendance: In an ongoing group, it is inevitable that group members will have to miss meetings at times. No one should feel guilty for doing this. On the other hand, everyone should know that the other group members are counting on them to show up. Someone who misses two meetings in a row will begin to lose track of what is happening in the other members' lives, and since confidentiality makes it difficult to catch up, it will be helpful if everyone will make the group a priority. However, support groups do work even if people come and go. *"Now that you have purified yourselves by obeying the truth so that you have sincere love for your brothers, love one another deeply, from the heart"* (1 Peter 1:22).

Open or Closed: Some support groups are open to all comers; new people may join at any time. Other groups feel freer to be honest when the membership remains stable for some length of time, so they open to new members only a few times a year. You can decide what works best for you.

Ownership: The group belongs to everyone in the group equally. Decisions should be made by consensus whenever possible. Everyone shares responsibility for the group and its goals. *"I appeal to you, brothers, in the name of our Lord Jesus Christ, that all of you agree with one another so that there may be no divisions among you and that you may be perfectly united in mind and thought"* (1 Corinthians 1:10).

Accountability: In the first few weeks, or after you have been through *The Financial Planning Workbook,* each of you should set some personal goals for where you want to be financially two years from now and how you are going to take steps with your budget to get there. *Accountability means you are giving permission for other members to hold you accountable for the goals you have set.* No one sets goals for you except you, but you let others help you stick to them. No one will be snooping into your private life; it will be up to you to tell people when you overspend in some area. *"Submit to one another out of reverence for Christ"* (Ephesians 5:21).

Accessibility: Ideally, you should give group members permission to call you whenever they need moral support or someone with whom to brainstorm ideas. Make clear any limits you want to place on your accessibility, such as "Please don't call me at work." Also, everyone should feel free to say so if someone calls at an inconvenient time.

Leadership: You will need to decide whether you will have one person guide your discussions each week or whether you will rotate leadership. It's best if one person takes responsibility for logistics (notifying people when meetings are moved or canceled, starting and stopping meetings on time, and so on). This need not be the discussion leader. Also, it's often good if someone other than the discussion leader hosts the group, handles refreshments, and so on. Sharing these responsibilities gives everyone ownership in the group.

Men Only?: Some men are uncomfortable talking openly about their finances in front of women. Also, men and women tend to talk about money differently. While there are many advantages to having couples together in one group, you may decide that it is better to have a men's group and a women's group, rather than to have some men drop out altogether. One strategy is to have men and women meet simultaneously in different rooms of a home or church so that couples can arrive together and socialize together afterward.

One could go on and on, but these are enough ground rules to spark your thinking. The group I have described here is intentionally flexible. It is not primarily designed to teach information but to provide a source of belonging and respect, other than what the world offers. It is an outpost of the kingdom of God, reflecting core kingdom values like the *"one another"* quoted in the previous verses.

If you are using this guide as part of an ongoing small group, you may not want to sidetrack your entire group to the agenda of debt for the next year. But do consider planning to check in with each other once a month to see how you are each doing with your process of becoming debt-free.

2. What is your initial reaction to the kind of group described here? What would be its pros and cons?

3. What would you like to get out of a group like this?

4. What risks would be involved? How would you
   address those risks?

5. Would you want to change any of the guidelines
   given above? How?

6. Can you think of any other guidelines you would like
   to add? What are they?

7. How could a group like this help you learn to distinguish needs from wants?

8. How could it help you flourish under sacrifice?

9. Would you want to be a part of this group? Why or why not?

The Grace Adventure

You would never have gotten this far without grace, and grace can get you the rest of the way. Close this session by allowing each participant to thank God for one thing he or she has received from this group. Then the leader can end by reading Ephesians 3:20–21: *"Now to him who is able to do immeasurably more than all we ask or imagine, according to his power that is at work within us, to him be glory in the church and in Christ Jesus throughout all generations, for ever and ever! Amen."*

*   *   *   *

"Preserve sound judgment and discernment, do not let them out of your sight; they will be life for you, an ornament to grace your neck. Then you will go on your way in safety, and your foot will not stumble. . . . The Lord will be your confidence and will keep your foot from being snared" (Proverbs 3:21–23, 26).

Christian Financial Concepts Inc.

Teaching | Biblical Principles of Managing Money

Larry Burkett, founder and president of Christian Financial Concepts, is the best-selling author of 51 books on business and personal finances and 2 novels. He also hosts two radio programs broadcast on hundreds of stations worldwide.

Larry holds degrees in marketing and finance, and for several years served as a manager in the space program at Cape Canaveral, Florida. He also has been vice president of an electronics manufacturing firm. Larry's education, business experience, and solid understanding of God's Word enable him to give practical, Bible-based financial counsel to families, churches, and businesses.

Founded in 1976, Christian Financial Concepts is a nonprofit, nondenominational ministry dedicated to helping God's people gain a clear understanding of how to manage their money according to scriptural principles. While practical assistance is provided on many levels, the purpose of CFC is simply *to bring glory to God by freeing His people from financial bondage so they may serve Him to their utmost.*

One major avenue of ministry involves the training of volunteers in budget and debt counseling and linking them with financially troubled families and individuals through a nationwide referral network. CFC also provides financial management seminars and workshops for churches and other groups. (Formats available include audio, video, video with moderator, and live instruction.) A full line of printed and audio-visual materials related to money management is available through CFC's materials department (1-800-722-1976).

Career Pathways, another outreach of Christian Financial Concepts, helps teenagers and adults find their occupational calling. The Career Pathways "Testing Package" gauges a person's work priorities, skills, vocational interests, and personality. Reports in each of these areas define a person's strengths, weaknesses, and unique, God-given pattern for work.

For further information about the ministry of Christian Financial Concepts, write to:

Christian Financial Concepts
PO Box 2377
Gainesville, Georgia 30503-2377

OTHER BOOKS BY LARRY BURKETT
Available at your local bookstore

The Financial Planning Workbook

This workbook includes practical advice about managing your finances and provides a series of easy-to-follow worksheets that allow you to structure and maintain your family's budget. Larry shows you where to start, how to stay on track, and even addresses special budgeting problems. Extra worksheets are included.

The Word on Finances

This useful tool contains a collection of relevant Scriptures arranged under eight comprehensive headings. Larry's practical wisdom opens each of the more than seventy topical selections.

Debt-Free Living

This book is for anyone whose money ran out before the month did. Again! Or even if your financial situation hasn't reached a crisis point, you will benefit from Larry's wise counsel. Through case studies of several marriages helped through proper financial counsel, Larry shows how to become and remain debt-free. He warns about the kinds of credit to avoid and provides specific how-to's for solving debt problems. *Debt-Free Living* remains a best-seller, with more than 150,000 copies in print.

How to Manage Your Money

There is so much religious "folklore" regarding money that few Christians understand God's true will in finances. But the Scriptures have plenty to say about how we should handle the funds entrusted to us. There are more than 700 direct references to money in the Bible and hundreds more indirect references. *How to Manage Your Money*, a Bible study by Larry Burkett, brings many of these references to light as it introduces Christians to the "scriptural" view of finances. This workbook covers such topics as stewardship, short- and long-range planning, tithing, and much more.

Your Finances in Changing Times

With more than a million copies in print, this book is a perfect introduction to basic financial management. It is a complete money guide, offering biblical concepts and practical suggestions for building a sound financial program. Learn to plan for the future, get out or stay out of debt, and much more.

Moody Press, a ministry of Moody Bible Institute,
is designed for education, evangelization, and edification.
If we may assist you in knowing more about Christ
and the Christian life, please write us without obligation:
Moody Press, c/o MLM, Chicago, Illinois 60610.